12.00

D0569077

CÉZANNE

P. Cezanne

BY YVON TAILLANDIER

CROWN PUBLISHERS, INC. - NEW YORK

Title page: CÉZANNE WITH A BOWLER HAT, 1883-1887
Oil on canvas, 17⅛″ × 14″ (44.5 × 35.5 cm)
Ny Carlsberg Glyptotek, Copenhagen

Collection published under the direction of:
MADELEINE LEDIVELEC-GLOECKNER

ISBN 0-517-03717-3

PRINTED IN ITALY – INDUSTRIE GRAFICHE CATTANEO S.P.A., BERGAMO
© 1977 BONFINI PRESS CORPORATION, NAEFELS, SWITZERLAND
NEW REVISED EDITION

THE ASS AND THE THIEVES.   Oil on canvas, 16⅛″ × 21⅞″ (41 × 55 cm)
Galleria d'Arte Moderna, Milan

CÉZANNE AND OUR AGE

A man in a bowler hat sauntered along the street.   He was dressed in a frock coat and carried a picture under his arm.   He walked around a block of buildings. Perhaps he had some premonition?   Suddenly he raised his head and looked over his shoulder.   It was then that the children started throwing stones at him.   One is staggered when one recalls who this man was.   Very few names survive their bearers.   Among these elect, these magic names, are great men of action and great

Portrait of Camille Pissarro
in Front of an Easel (Detail)
Private collection

artists. And the man in the bowler hat was one of these. Moreover, he sensed it: "A painter like me — there is only one every other century." In fact, he was modest in his claims, for there had not been a painter like him for more than two centuries. He was born at Aix-en-Provence, in 1839. He was to die in the same town in 1906. His name was Paul Cézanne.

Paul Cézanne: for millions of people today these two words stand for genius and painting. They also evoke a prodigious man, at once a father figure and a brother: A father figure because of the countless 20th century painters — Fauves, Cubists, Cubist-Fauves — who are largely indebted to him for that life-force that is style; a brother too, an artist who seems to belong to our century while he spent most of his life in the 19th century. At least he appears to have anticipated our time to an astonishing extent. He knew, however, the misery of being unappreciated and despised, as in the anecdote of his being stoned by some children, which Rainer Maria Rilke told in his "Briefe über Cézanne." Yet, when one retraces the story of his life, one realized that he enjoyed great advantages, that this father of modern painting — as he is often called — was a privileged son, and that this master began by being an excellent pupil, albeit not in art school. The details are significant. The son of a banker, he owed to his father's money an excellent classical education and the freedom, throughout his life, from financial worries. He knew Greek and Latin literature, even that of the decadence. In all likelihood, he had read the Greek prose writer Lucian and the Alexandrian epic poet Apollonius Rhodius, both of whom tell the story of a man who was changed into an ass and captured by thieves. He demonstrated this knowledge of the Classics when he painted *The Ass and the Thieves* (see

p. 5).   But this leaden sky and murky sea, this wind rushing through dark foliage, these muscular robbers dressed in red or blue, this strange figure smoking a pipe or a cigar (one cannot tell which, and it is an anachronism anyway), this pathetic little white ass, of which one can see little more than the hindquarters — this is an imaginary world which Cézanne could only have seen in dreams inspired by literature.   It could be said that this twilight, this chiaroscuro, are found in the work of painters that the young Cézanne admired — the followers of Caravaggio shown at the Aix Museum.

These people, trees, and shattered rocks are recollections of pictures that he had once contemplated.   But what a world of difference between his models and his painting!   These human bodies, for example, all muscles, thick-set, and squat, have unnatural proportions. They are not to be found in pictures or life.   And in this sense, Cézanne had never really seen them.   He seems almost an initiator who created a world out of next to nothing, out of fragments of memories, vague reveries. This creator *ex nihilo* thought he was a god.

"They think they are gods!"   How often has one heard this charge leveled at painters of today?   In all that part of his work for which one can level the same charge at Cézanne — if "charge" is the right word — Cézanne was a pioneer and more: Born earlier, indeed much earlier, he is nevertheless a kind of brother to the painters of today.   But it is not only this winging fantasy, so very much in evidence in modern painting, which first appeared in the work of Cézanne. Ours is a tragic age, torn between hope and despair, peace and war. Its anguish is expressed in the work of some painters, where light and shade struggle like life and death, cheerfulness and despondency, as in Cézanne's *The Ass and the Thieves*. This tragic chiaroscuro of contemporary painting is present — and with the same violence — in nearly all of Cézanne's early pictures: *Still Life with Black Clock* (see p. 12), *The Negro Scipio* (see p. 10), or *Still Life with Skull* (see p. 37).

Our age is dazzled by the power of man over matter and the power of matter itself. It has its painters who have made pictorial matter — the thickness and texture of color — the symbol of this power. The thick layers of paint, like enormous muscles, evoke the idea of force. But when the lover of modern painting considers these strange pictures covered with layers of paint or some other media of varying thickness, pictures that have an almost three-dimensional quality, he should not let himself imagine that he has just discovered something new in art: Some paintings by Cézanne already feature such texture, notably *Uncle Dominique* (see p. 9) and *Portrait of Victor Chocquet* (see p. 17).

*Portrait of Madame Cézanne
Leaning on Her Elbow
Private collection*

A new world emerges, filled by weird machines and extended by a vastly developed science. Our age takes its shape under its eyes. Our age believes we need a new man for this new world. Scientists, writers, and artists search for such a new man, they look for a new face and a new body. Cézanne also looked

UNCLE DOMINIQUE, 1865-1866.   Oil on canvas, 31⅜″ × 25¼″ (79.7 × 64.1 cm)
The Metropolitan Museum of Art, New York
Wolfe Fund. Acquisition from the Museum of Modern Art. Collection Lizzie P. Bliss

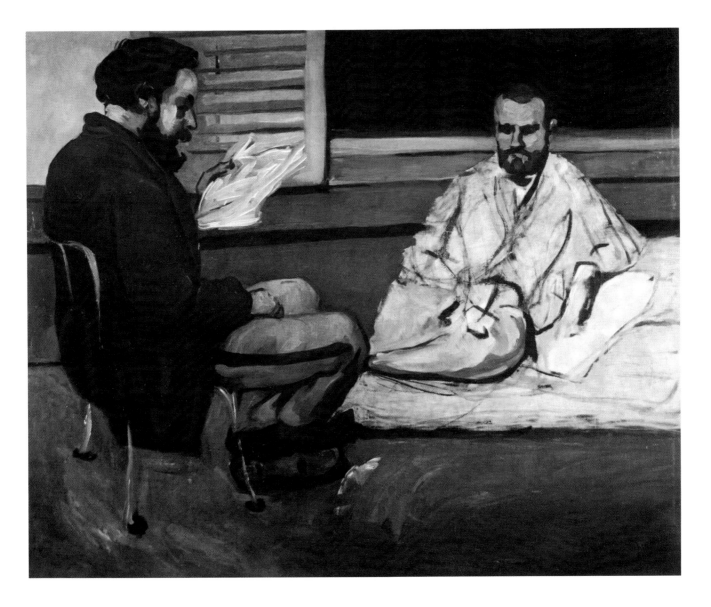

◁

The Negro Scipio, ca 1867
Oil on canvas, 42⅛″ × 32⅝″ (107 × 83 cm)
Museu de Arte, São Paulo, Brazil

Paul Alexis Reading to Zola, 1869-1870
Oil on canvas, 20½″ × 22″ (52 × 55.9 cm)
Private collection, New York

11

STILL LIFE WITH BLACK CLOCK, 1869-1871
Oil on canvas, 21⅝″ × 29½″ (55 × 75 cm)
Private collecion

for him. Let the lover of modern painting examine, for example, the bodies of the thieves in the bottom left of *The Ass and the Thieves*. He will find extraordinary proportions and rubbery suppleness that scarcely correspond to the classical canon of anatomy. The arm of *The Boy in a Red Jacket* (see p. 32) is unnaturally long, quite abnormal, and, once again, there is the strange rubbery suppleness. The *Harlequin's* head (see p. 64) features an extraordinarily enlarged upper-lip and a chin so atrophied that it disappears altogether. In *The Large Bathers* (see p. 81), the woman on the extreme left had enormous legs and thighs, a chest tapered like a cone, and a tiny head like an insect's. The lover of modern art will find

in every case the prelude to that mangling of anatomy, heedless of monstrosities, which characterizes the experiments of Cubists, Expressionists, Naifs, and Abstract Anthropomorphists, of artists conjuring up, more or less consciously, a new man as different from the old as the new world is different from the old world.

Ours is an age of change. An astonishingly short time suffices to change the face of a city. The countryside is sprawled over by the towns and becomes a bawling factory. The sky itself, once thought impregnable, can now be penetrated. Societies collapse, hierarchies crumble. One generation follows the next — but each one is different. A simple surgical operation will change a person's sex. We no longer know what we are. Everything is fluid — as in some modern paintings where trees resemble women's bodies, where

Rococo Clock, ca 1900
Pencil, 8⅜" × 5⅜" (21.4 × 13.1 cm)
Kupferstichkabinett, Basel

13

Study for The Autopsy, ca 1865. Charcoal, 11½" × 16¾" (31 × 48.6 cm)
The Art Institute, Chicago. Mr. and Mrs. Tiffany Blake Fund

the outline of a landscape suggests an animal or a human creature. Cézanne too plays with nature. He plasters the face of *Victor Chocquet* with a green vegetation more like grass than skin. The sky in his landscapes is like a wall, the air is transformed into stone. In his *Bathers under a Bridge* (see p. 42), the women are like bushes. If *The Boy in a Red Jacket* does not have a rubber arm, then he has liana sprouting from his shoulder.

Ours is an age that likes to probe the most intimate secrets. The anonymous crowd bores us. We seek avidly to know individuals, to isolate them from the mass, to discover their most instinctive reactions. That is why there exists a school of painting today that lays bare the painter's most basic impulses and to all that it strives to evoke, adds the flattering illusion that viewer and painter know each other so well that they are one and the same person. This kind of painting, which reveals the most inward self and encourages participation, is called "action painting." And this action painting, which is hailed as a great novelty, is to be found in Cézanne's work. Look, for example, at the picture he painted in 1869, entitled *Paul Alexis Reading to Zola* (see p. 11). Look at Zola's white jacket and the manner it is painted: heavy brush strokes, thick lines, slashes, and stripes, revealing Cézanne's holy fury and fervor. It seems to speak to us, surely. Our imagination is fired, we can actually see Cézanne at work. We stand behind him, we follow his gestures and, what is more, have the impression that we are making them with him. We are in a creative trance. We share his fury and joy in tracing lines, making them cross and zigzag, making them sometimes light and barely visible, sometimes heavy, wide, and deep. And we are with him when he daubs blotches, splashes, and streams of color. Paul Alexis's manuscript creates the same effect. This is already "action painting." Is this a picture out of the past or the present? We do not know. Judging by the characteristics we have just discovered, it resembles so many paintings shown in today's galleries and museums.

And how many paintings one sees today! How many images! How many photographs! How many landscapes, simulated or real! Television, the cinema, and travel bombard our eyes and mind with forms and colors. How tired our eyes become! But some modern painters have taken this into account and have hit on an extremely sparse style of painting. Few colors and scanty lines, a few blotches and streaks, hardly anything. Another fad, you say. But no. Some ancient Chinese painters reduced their picture to a few diaphanous spots. But it is not necessary to go back to ancient China to find examples of similar economy of means. Some of Cézanne's watercolors, such as *House in Provence* (see p. 45), are cases in point.

A SENSE OF MASS WEIGHT

I remember one day, when having looked long at a small still life by Cézanne representing a few apples and a vase of flowers, which was on show at the Louvre — it is now to be seen at the Musée d'Orsay — I went into the sculpture

PORTRAIT OF VICTOR CHOCQUET, 1876-1877
Oil on canvas
18⅛″ × 14⅛″ (46 × 35.9 cm)
Private collection ▷

Portrait of Achille Empereire, ca 1868
Charcoal
Kupferstichkabinett, Basel

Profile of a Man
Pencil
Kupferstichkabinett, Basel

16

◁
FARMYARD AT AUVERS, ca 1879-1880
Oil on canvas, 25⅝″ × 21¼″ (65 × 54 cm)
Musée d'Orsay, Paris

HARVESTERS RESTING, 1880
Oil on canvas
Private collection

19

THE PLATE OF APPLES, 1878-1879
Oil on canvas, 17⅞″ × 21⅝″ (45.5 × 55 cm)
Collection: Mr. and Mrs. Walter Annenberg
Palm Springs, California

rooms.   There I stopped in front of a wild beast with a human head.   It was
the finest of the Egyptian sphinxes.   This sculpture expressed all the mysteries
of Egypt — and they are doubtless the mysteries of life.   I had exactly the
same impression as I had a minute earlier when standing before the small still
life.   What did these two works have in common?   They are separated by a great
many centuries, differences in technique — one being a sculpture, the other a
painting — and themes — the sphinx being a monster laden with symbols, the
still life representing everyday objects and apparently devoid of all mysticism.
They have much in common, however, and two things in particular. First of all,
there is their enigmatic quality.   I do not know whether this quality makes me
see the sphinx as a lion or a man.   Does it have man's wisdom or the lion's fury?
It is impossible to tell.   Just as when I compared Cézanne's apples and vase of
flowers, I could not decide whether the apples had the brittle hardness of

Sketch Sheet with Bathers, 1897-1900.   Pencil and watercolor.   Kupferstichkabinett, Basel

Study after Benedetto da Maiano
Filippo Strozzi, 1881-1884
Pencil, 8⅜″ × 0⅜″ (21.4 × 13.1 cm)
Kupferstichkabinett, Basel

earthenware or the juicy softness of fruit. Today one asks oneself similar questions about the figures in abstract paintings. What do they weigh? What are they made of? What do they represent? And again one can find no answer. This enigmatic quality of Cézanne's works and of abstract paintings corresponds to one of the needs of our age. In the past, when faith was stronger and less vague, man's final destiny was depicted. Today, man's destiny is an enigma. Will mankind destroy itself, or perpetuate itself in the form of Superman? We do not know. But although this ignorance is rather alarming for man, who regards himself as superior to other beings because he can look ahead, he likes searching for images and objects expressing his perplexity. Through them, he develops his imagination and creativity, with the aid of which he hopes to find the key to the enigma.

The second characteristic common to Cézanne's still life and the sphinx eluded me for a long time. I kept telling myself that there was a similarity of style between them. The solution, however, was simpler. Like the man with a long experience in spiritual struggle who was amazed to see the hard mask of a soldier on the face of a nun, I realized, one day, that while Cézanne was one of the greatest painters of all time, he had the mind of a sculptor. I should not have been surprised, since I already knew that I should expect anything from Cézanne. The sphinx and the still life had this in common: Both were the work of men who were essentially sculptors. One had expressed himself in stone; the other,

Woman Reading. Private collection

Landscape with Trees.   Pencil.   Private collection

indirectly, through pictures.   Unlike several of his contemporaries — Auguste Renoir, Edgar Degas, Paul Gauguin — Cézanne never took up sculpting, but there is no denying that he had the sculptor's feeling for mass-weight.   Moreover, he said himself, quite categorically, "What counts is only mass."   Indeed, this sense of the solidity of things can be explained in terms of our relationship with works of art.   The first function of a work of art is to draw attention to itself. Now an impression of solid weight is a surprise in a painting.   One is surprised that there should be relief on a flat surface.   And so one's attention is caught and held — and nothing is more significant in a picture. The importance that Cézanne attached to mass-weight proves therefore that he realized this.   But there were other reasons for his interest in volume, reasons rooted in his own character.   His biographers all agree that he was shy, lacked self-confidence, and felt that he was weak.   Volume suggests might and Cézanne may have felt a surge of strength when creating volume in his paintings.

Cézanne was born three years after the invention of the telegraph and five years after that of the propeller — at the beginning of the technical, scientific, and industrial revolution that was to change radically our world and confer on man such vast power over the universe. Cézanne's interest in the three-dimensional may have been a desire to express this power that man was beginning to acquire. There is also the fact that he came from the Mediterranean. In that sunny land, the light is so bright that it erases color. Volume and not color make things seem real. So volume had to be the touch-stone of reality in Cézanne's pictures. When he painted from imagination, as in *The Ass and the Thieves*, he needed volume to give substance to his dreams.

More than a sense of the solidity of things is needed to reproduce that solidity in a picture. In his early days Cézanne used several methods that seemed to satisfy him. The strangest one was the use of an actual relief to create the illusion of a greater relief. Hence his textured paintings. He also used the outline of

Landscape with Bare Trees. Pencil, 5″ × 8¾″ (12.7 × 22.2 cm) (Sheet). Sketchbook The Art Institute, Chicago

shapes, making it round to suggest spherical volumes, without flat surface. In this he is close to Michelangelo — after whom he executed many drawings — Rubens, Delacroix, and, in a more general way, the Baroque painters. The most effective method he adopted, and an entirely traditional one, was the juxtaposing of deep shade and bright light, in other words the contrast of chiaroscuro.

L'Amour de Puget, ca 1888
Drawing
The Brooklyn Museum, New York

These contrasts can be traced back to the Aix Museum and its pictures by followers of Caravaggio. They also belonged to the visual background of Cézanne's childhood. Many Mediterranean people shy away from the blinding light and overwhelming heat. Their house is often dark in broad daylight. A ray of sunshine may pierce this daytime night, and its brilliance is all the more intense because it is isolated. And this light shining through shade is nothing less than chiaroscuro. Cézanne thus used chiaroscuro to depict an aspect of a world that was familiar to him. But he also realized that when reproduced in paint, it became extraordinarily powerful: chiaroscuro — in its simplest form, the contrast of black and white — is the most striking contrast a painter can achieve. It is the contrast of light and its very opposite. No contrasts of colors can be so sharp, for light contains all colors. One realizes this when one sees light broken down into colors in a prism or a rainbow. Black does not appear then: It belongs to another world, that of darkness. The contrast of black and white is so strong that even when they are separated by a gray zone, or tinted to be brought closer together, it is still stronger than any contrast of colors. It is so striking that it cannot fail to attract attention. This is the first and most significant result of chiaroscuro. The second result is that it produces an effect of depth and relief. The difference between black and white is such that one cannot imagine they are on the same plane, the same level. One of them seems withdrawn in relation to the other, seems to stand back. This is how the illusion of depth is created, suggesting different planes and relief. The impression of depth must be controlled, however, to avoid serious drawbacks.

There is the risk that one will see nothing but relief in the picture. Seen from a distance, it will become a window behind which a solid mass can be seen. One will no longer think it is a painting at all. The mass-weight will cease to hit us and the surprise value will be lost. Another drawback

Naked Man Standing with Arms Raised, Back View
Pencil
Private collection

lies in the fact that this same contrast, which produces the illusion of volume, has its own fascination. One sees nothing else. One's eyes remain glued to it, unable to move on to the other parts of the picture. One cannot see the whole picture and one feels frustrated.

In the first ten years of his career as a painter, when he was using chiaroscuro, Cézanne understood perfectly the drawbacks of too sharp a contrast. He strove to remedy it and he succeeded. In order to preserve the effect of surprise created by a mass seeming to jut out on the flat surface of a picture, he painted flat surfaces running parallel to the mass and resembling the background of a bas-relief. In *The Negro Scipio*, the figure seems to be leaning against a white screen. In *Paul Alexis Reading to Zola*, there is the wall of the house and the shutters. In *The Ass and the Thieves*, there is the rock-terrace, as flat and vertical as a wall. So that the solid masses and the contrasts they produce would not be too overwhelming, Cézanne trained himself to work the solid masses into the flat parts, like enamels set in metal. The solid masses seem bound to the surface, and the eye glides from the masses to the background. In *Paul Alexis Reading to Zola*, the eye moves from Zola's white jacket to the white cushions lying against the wall, and from the verticality of the cushions to that of the wall. It also moves from Paul Alexis's hair to a more shaded part of the shutters. In *The Ass and the Thieves*, it moves from the blue of the sea to the dark shades in the

Landscape with Trees. Pencil, 5″ × 8¾″ (12.7 × 22.2 cm) (Sheet) Sketchbook. The Art Institute, Chicago

28

▷

VASE OF FLOWERS, 1873-1875
Oil on canvas, 16⅛″ × 10⅝″ (41 × 27cm)
Musée d'Orsay, Paris

A MAN IN A STRAW HAT - PORTRAIT OF BOYER, 1870-1871
Oil on canvas, 21⅝″ × 15¼″ (55 × 38.8 cm)
The Metropolitan Museum of Art, New York
Collection H.O. Havemeyer. Gift of Mrs. H.O. Havemeyer

PORTRAIT OF THE ARTIST, 1879-1882
Oil on canvas
24¼″ × 19¾″ (61.5 × 50.5 cm)
Kunstmuseum, Bern

BOY IN A RED JACKET, 1890-1895.   Oil on canvas, 36¼″ × 28¾″ (92 × 73 cm)
Emil G. Buehrle Foundation, Zurich

thieves' bodies, and from the whiteness of the ass to the scarcely visible golden sand. In the portrait of *Uncle Dominique* (see p. 9), it moves from the light blue in the background to the pink of the face or from the yellowish dressing gown to the dark blue background, both executed in thick layers of paint shaped by the knife-edge.

These links between various parts of a picture — links balancing the fragmentation created by contrasts — make the solid masses seem welded to the surface on which they appear; the connection with the surface has not been severed, and the eye cannot wander around the masses. One's mind does not wander from Uncle Dominique, from the thieves about to steal the ass, from Emile Zola or Paul Alexis, or from any of the figures or objects in Cézanne's pictures. One cannot stroll around them, so to speak, as one strolls around a statue — the *Victory of Samothrace* (Musée du Louvre, Paris) or, indeed, any other statue. It is that which, from the beginning, distinguished Cézanne's work from classical painting. He admired classical painters: "I want to be the Poussin of nature." But there was always a difference between them — and it is a significant one: Classical painting resembles sculpture in the round, while Cézanne's work creates an illusion of bas-relief. He said, "A painter like me — there is only one every other century." And in a sense, one has to go back much further than two centuries to find one.

Man Reading. Pencil
Private collection

The Village of L'Estaque. Pencil and watercolor
Museum of Art, Rhode Island School of Design, Providence

El Greco lived a little more than two centuries before Cézanne (1548-1625), and he was the only classical artist that could be compared to him. He too had conceived of a style that greatly reduced depth and established a thousand strong links between the solid masses and the background, producing the overall effect of a bas-relief. But Greco, whom Cézanne admired and one of whose paintings he copied, had no successor. He had a few pupils, but no disciples to carry on his work. He was such an accident in the history of art that he was forgotten soon after his death. Only two centuries later was he rediscovered. And then there was Cézanne. No, the painter who most resembles Cézanne, both as regards style and historical role, is Giotto (1266-1336). Both artists saw painting as a bas-relief. And they were both on the brink of a new era in painting. In the Middle Ages, Giotto was the forerunner of Renaissance art; Cézanne ushered in modern painting. Cézanne said it himself, to Emile Bernard, "I am the primitive of the way that I discovered." Giotto's words were not preserved for posterity, but he could have said the same thing. He put an end to a period

Two Trees. Pencil. Private collection

when painting was totally separate from sculpture, with no relief nor depth. Giotto brought about a revolution by introducing the illusion of bas-relief. This revolution led to the illusion of sculpture in the round in the Renaissance painters and their successors, until Cézanne rediscovered Giotto's bas-relief. Cézanne and Giotto are the two ends of a period spanning nearly six centuries. This is why Cézanne's work marks a decisive point in the history of art. He would not have such significance, however, had he not been born in the 19th century and met the Impressionists. These circumstances made a Greco of Cézanne — a Greco who had his place in the history of art but also helped to shape it.

RELIEF THROUGH COLOR

The scene is Paris, the café Guerbois, which was to become famous. A group of men are arguing fiercely. One of them, about thirty, has a recognizable southern

Still Life with Candlestick, 1881-1884. Pencil, 4¹⁵/₁₆″ × 7¾″ (12.5 × 19.6 cm)
Kupferstichkabinett, Basel

STILL LIFE WITH SKULL, ca 1865
Oil on canvas, 18½″ × 24⅝″ (47.5 × 62.5 cm)
Private collection, Zurich

THE CARDPLAYERS, 1890-1892
Oil on canvas, 25½″ × 32″ (64.7 × 81.2 cm)
The Metropolitan Museum of Art, New York
Gift of Stephen C. Clark

The Cardplayers, 1893-1896
Oil on canvas
17¾″ × 22½″ (45 × 57 cm)
Musée d'Orsay, Paris

THE SEINE AT BERCY (after ARMAND GUILLAUMIN), 1876-1878
Oil on canvas, 23¼″ × 28⅜″ (59 × 72 cm)
Kunsthalle, Hamburg

accent.   This is Cézanne.   The others were to be later known as Impressionists when, in 1874, they exhibited in the rooms of the photographer Nadar.   A year before the exhibition, Cézanne was working with a typical Impressionist, Camille Pissarro, at Auvers-sur-Oise.   Pissarro taught him to paint without black.   For Cézanne, this was to be both a catastrophe and a source of strength.   It was a catastrophe because Cézanne needed to paint relief; black produces sharp contrasts, which in turn create powerful masses and relief.   Deprived of black, Cézanne was robbed of his power.   But he had fallen in love with color.

In 1886, he married Hortense Fiquet, a model he had first met in 1869.   They had one son.   This marriage, however, had less effect on his art than a much earlier marriage with color.   What, then, excited this passion?   First the fact that color was part of the optimism of this last quarter of the 19th century, an optimism born from science, which was supposed to bring a solution to all problems of mankind.   Science and color met in the work of the physicist Eugène Chevreul.   They both stood for this end of the 19th century.   Even more striking was the fact that the optimism aroused by science found its symbol in color — light color freed from black.   Cézanne had absorbed the spirit of his time, like his childhood friend, Zola, who was the theoretician of a literature that strove to be scientific.   He could not have been a stranger to this spirit of enthusiasm, hence his passion for color.   There were also other reasons, and a technical one in particular.   Since colors produce less striking contrasts than black and

Sketch for The Cardplayers, 1890-1892
Pencil and watercolor
Museum of Art
Rhode Island School of Design, Providence
Gift of Mrs. Murray S. Danforth

BATHERS UNDER A BRIDGE, ca 1900
Watercolor and pencil on white paper, 8¼″ × 10¾″ (21 × 27.4)
The Metropolitan Museum of Art, New York
Maria de Witt Jesup Fund
Acquisition from the Museum of Modern Art
Collection Lillie P. Bliss

THE STRUGGLE OF LOVE, 1875-1876
Pencil, watercolor, and gouache
5⅞″ × 8⅝″ (15 × 22 cm)
Private collection, Zurich

white, they can soften perspective, limit depth, and create a kind of space where the distant seems near — in other words, the same kind of space as that of bas-relief. However, bas-relief means three dimensions. Cézanne's marriage with color meant a marriage of color and volume. Is such a marriage possible? It is very difficult, but not impossible. And herein lie the courage and tenacity of Cézanne. The chance that such a marriage would succeed was slim. Cézanne risked everything in the cause of bringing off this slim chance.

One feature of the Impressionists' technique caused great surprise and aroused much discussion: their use of purple in suggesting shadows. To an eye unaccustomed to the Impressionist vision, the shadows that appear in broad daylight are gray, if not black. This the Impressionists regarded as an error. They were of the opinion that everything one sees in the open air and in daylight is light — even the shadows. Consequently, shadows should be some color other than gray, for gray is, after all, a watered-down black, a pale reminder of night shadows. But why purple? Because purple, like blue and green, is one of the so-called "cool" colors, less stimulating to the eye than such "warm" colors as

View of Val-Harmé, near Auvers. Pencil. Private collection

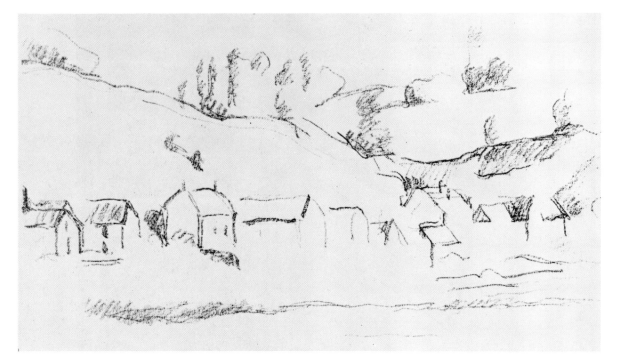

HOUSE IN PROVENCE, ca 1890
Pencil and watercolor
16¾″ × 22½″ (42.5 × 57 cm)
Private collection

Men Around a Woman.   Pencil, 5″ × 8¾″ (12.7 × 22.2 cm) (Sheet)
Sketchbook.   The Art Institute, Chicago

yellow, orange, and red.   These cool colors have a calming effect, they suggest sleep and darkness while not belonging to the night.   They can therefore replace effectively gray and black, which are restful colors.

If colors could replace — at least to a certain extent — black and gray, they could produce relief and give the illusion of volume.   The other Impressionists were aware of this, but they cared more for atmosphere than volume and never really explored the possibilities of this discovery.   Cézanne, however, explored them to the limit.   This was his slim chance to reconcile his sculptor's spirit with his passion for color, the clearest examples of which can be found in his watercolors.

Is *House in Provence* (see p. 45) in ruins?   Is the blue in the window frame and the arched porch the blue of the sky?   It is only a shadow suggesting openings in the wall.   The bathers in *Bathers under a Bridge* (see p. 42) are not swimming in an autumnal river and the yellow in the trees is not that of dead leaves; it is just a warm color intended to bring out other parts of the foliage.   The blue halo around the fruit and earthenware pot in *Apples, Carafe, and Sugar Bowl* (see p. 67) is not smoke.   It is a cool color to highlight the warm colors of the most three-dimensional parts of the painting.   This relief is rather weak, because color is less effective in creating a three-dimensional effect.   Could the sculptor's spirit that was in Cézanne be satisfied with it?   Such relief was sufficient for watercolors, in which shapes were mere hints.   But oil paintings must reach beyond hints and Cézanne needed more powerful means.

In 1905, a year before Cézanne's death, a group of young artists exhibited a few paintings that earned them the name of Fauves, on account of the savage violence of their colors.   They embraced one of Paul Gauguin's axioms: "If a tree trunk looks slightly red to you, paint it bright red."   But Gauguin was younger than Cézanne, who said of him: "He took my little sensation over all the world's seas." The Fauves knew how much Gauguin was indebted to Cézanne, hence, indirectly,

Bathers.   Pencil.   Private collection

◁

THE GATE AT CHANTILLY, 1888
Pencil, gouache, and watercolor, 7¾″ × 4⅝″ (19.6 × 11.7 cm)
Smith College Museum of Art, Northampton, Massachusetts
Gift of the Adele R. Levy Fund

BATHERS IN FRONT OF A TENT, 1885
Oil on canvas
25½″ × 31¾″ (64.8 × 80.7 cm)
Private collection

STILL LIFE WITH ONIONS, 1896-1898
Oil on canvas
26″ × 32¼″ (66 × 82 cm)
Musée d'Orsay, Paris

Flowers and Fruit, 1888-1890
Oil on canvas
25⅝″ × 31⅞″ (65 × 81 cm)
Nationalmuseum, Berlin

51

GREEN APPLES, 1873
Oil on canvas
10¼″ × 12⅝″ (26 × 32 cm)
Musée d'Orsay, Paris

THE GREEN PITCHER, 1885-1887
Pencil and watercolor
8⅝″ × 9¾″ (22 × 24.7 cm)
Musée du Louvre, Cabinet des Dessins, Paris

what they owed to him. Among the most significant Fauves, Dufy painted several Cézanne-like pictures and Matisse owned for a long time Cézanne's *Bathers*. When compared to Cézanne's paintings, however, the Fauves' pictures strike by their lack of relief. The Fauves only used colors to evoke rounded surfaces, while Cézanne used also other techniques. He had four ways of increasing the three-dimensional effect. The first consisted in making some concessions to classical technique; the second, in the breaking up of the mass; the third, in reducing masses into simple geometric shapes; and the fourth, in the treatment of perspective.

Bathers, ca 1890. Lithograph

The Eternal Feminine, 1870-1875. Pencil, 7″ × 9¼″ (17.7 × 23.6 cm)
Kupferstichkabinett, Basel

One is tempted to believe that Cézanne, like the Fauves, shaped masses essentially through color, because this is his favored technique. The results can be surprising. Bluebeard is a fairy tale monster, but the *Portrait of Madame Cézanne* (see p. 63) may lead to suppose that she belonged to the same race of monsters. She has blue eyebrows, blue on her cheeks, blue in her right ear, green in her left ear, and blue where nostril and cheek meet. Why? Because blue and green are necessary for creating three dimensions through color. *Victor Chocquet* (see p. 17), the first collector of Cézanne's work — he started in 1876, when the public had nothing but scorn for Cézanne — was not of the

SEATED MAN, 1900-1902. Pencil and watercolor, 18½″ × 14″ (47 × 35.5 cm)
Collection: John R. Gaines, Lexington, Kentucky

THE CHESTNUT TREE LANE AT JAS DE BOUFFAN, 1890-1895
Pencil and watercolor, 19¼″ × 12⅝″ (48.5 × 32 cm). Private collection, Switzerland

Mardi-Gras.   Pencil.   Private collection

Bluebeard family, but his beard is strangely green.   Why this extraordinary color?   Again, to create relief.

These peculiarities should not mislead into thinking that Cézanne limited himself to this technique.   Moreover, he took great liberties when using it.   In *Apples and Inkwell* (see p. 66), the rounder part of some apples is green, while the shadows are red.   In other words, warmth is replaced by coolness, the order of colors is reversed.   Cézanne saw little difference.   What mattered was that the contrasts broke up the surface.   "In nature," he told Emile Bernard, "there is no such thing as line or modeling, there are only contrasts."   Indeed, but contrasts between colors are weaker than that of light and shade used in classical relief.   Most of the time Cézanne resisted to the temptation of shaping relief through classical contrast, but not always.   In *The Cardplayers* (see p. 38), there is a hint of black in the players' clothes, and the background in the other version of *The Cardplayers* is painted in a very dark red. So he sometimes gave in to the temptation, but he regretted it afterwards. Toward the end of his life, when he had become famous, Cézanne painted a portrait of his dealer, Ambroise Vollard (Musée du Petit-Palais, Paris). It is a very dark picture, recalling the chiaroscuro of his early days. Vollard sat a hundred and fifteen times (and left a famous record of this labor). In the end, Cézanne was satisfied only with the light shirt front. He was no more satisfied with another very fine portrait, *Old Woman with a Rosary* (1895-1896, National Gallery, London), which he left lying about in a leaky corner of his studio. Why such negligence? The portrait is very dark, and Cézanne may have felt that he had conceded too much to classical technique. He avoided

Studies. Pencil. Kupferstichkabinett, Basel

59

THE BAY OF L'ESTAQUE, 1878-1882
Pencil, watercolor, and gouache
11½″ × 17¹⁵⁄₁₆″ (29.1 × 45.5 cm)
Kunsthaus, Zurich

THE BAY OF MARSEILLES SEEN FROM L'ESTAQUE, 1883-1885
Oil on canvas, 28¾″ × 39½″ (73 × 100 cm)
The Metropolitan Museum of Art, New York
Collection H.O. Havemeyer
Gift of Mrs. H.O. Havemeyer

THE ARTIST'S SON PAUL, ca 1888.   Oil on canvas, 25¾″ × 21¼″ (65.3 × 54 cm)
The National Gallery of Art, Washington, D.C. Collection Chester Dale

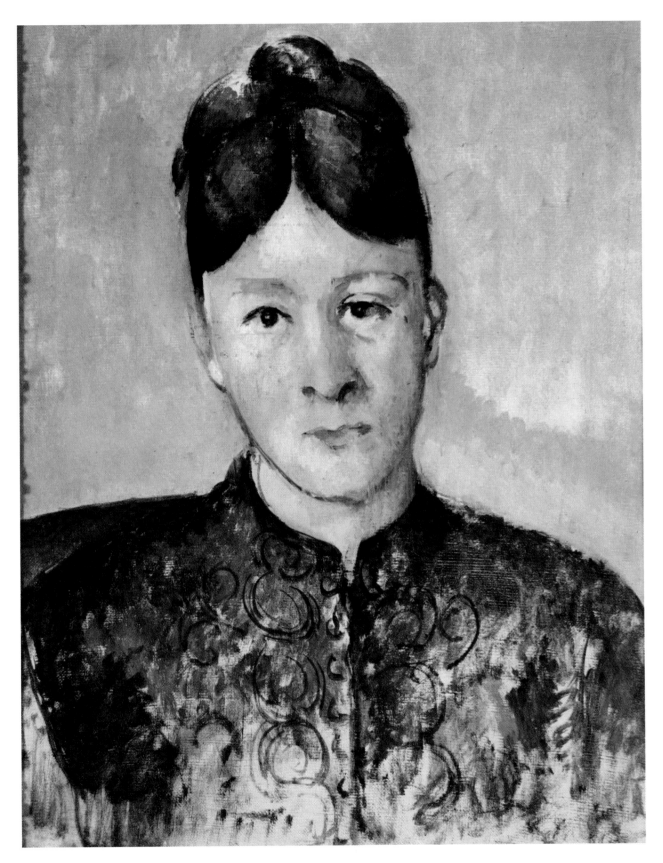

PORTRAIT OF MADAME CÉZANNE, ca 1885. Oil on canvas, 18⅛″ × 15″ (46 × 38 cm)
Private collection

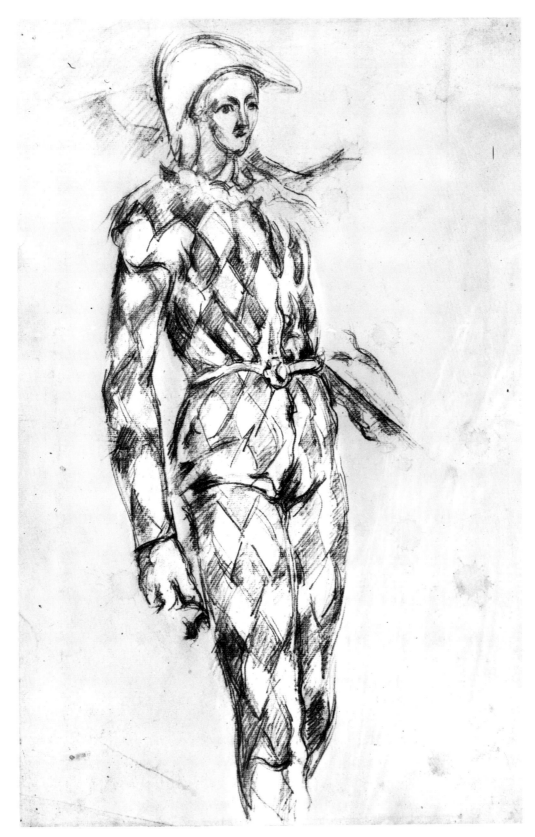

Harlequin, 1888
Pencil, 18⅝″ × 12³⁄₁₆″ (47.3 × 30.9 cm)
The Art Institute Chicago

◁
HARLEQUIN, 1888-1890
Oil on canvas, 36¼″ × 25½″ (92 × 65 cm)
Private collection

APPLES AND INKWELL, 1902-1906
Watercolor and pencil
12½" × 17¾" (31.7 × 45 cm)
Collection: Mr. and Mrs. Paul Hirschland
Great Neck, New York

APPLES, CARAFE, AND SUGARBOWL, ca 1900
Watercolor and pencil
18⅞″ × 24⅞″ (48 × 63 cm)
Kunsthistorisches Museum, Vienna

such concessions as often as possible. He looked for other ways of intensifying the impression of relief created by warm and cool colors, without darkening or clouding those colors. Since color contrast creates only weak relief, it should be applied to a surface commensurate with that weak power. It is difficult to suggest volume when painting on a large surface; conversely, it is easy on a small surface. A step of 1/8″ is imperceptible on a surface of three square feet; on a watch glass, it is enormous. Consequently, Cézanne fragmented his pictures, divided the masses into many smaller ones, for which the contrast of colors, weak as they are, suffice to evoke three-dimensional shape.

Portrait of Louis Guillaume
Dressed Up as a Pierrot
Pencil, 12⅜″ × 9⁹⁄₁₆″ (31.4 × 24.3 cm)
Kupferstichkabinett, Basel

The third technique was to have significant consequences. It consisted in reducing forms to simple geometric shapes, the solidity of which was evident. In a letter to Emile Bernard, dated April 15, 1904, Cézanne claimed "to treat nature by means of the cylinder, the sphere, and the cone..." When the contour of a form is simple like that of a geometric shape, the eye is not distracted from its mass-weight. By contrast, some shellfish, solid as they may be, give not the slightest impression of solidity, because the eye is so taken up following the winding maze of their contour. Sometimes, the human face seems as complicated as one of these shells, and Cézanne did not hesitate to simplify it. Look at *Girl with Doll* (see p. 84). The doll's head is reduced to a mere ball and the little girl has lost her mouth and most of her nose; her eyes are barely sketched in.

Carnival. Pencil. Private collection

Cézanne's apples are almost as famous as Adam and Eve's, but he did not paint that fruit so often to remind us of the cause of all our woes. He painted them because an apple is almost a sphere. For the same reason, he was partial to rotund earthenware and bowler hats. Clothes were often a pretext for geometric designs. The player on the left of *The Cardplayers* (see p. 39) combines fragments of spheres and cylinders that make him resemble a robot.

In 1908, two years after Cézanne's death, Georges Braque and Pablo Picasso showed their first Cubist paintings. The Cubists carried Cézanne's geometric treatment of nature to an extreme. Cézanne never went as far as they did, nor as far as the Cubists' successors — the geometric Abstractionists, in particular, who gave pride of place to shapes drawn with ruler and compass and regarded clarity of contour as one of the greatest artistic virtues. On the contrary, toward the end of his life, when he was in what Bernard Dorival called his baroque period, Cézanne exclaimed: "Contour escapes me." Indeed, this contradiction, which made him turn to geometry and also feel attracted by nature's rich confusion, is not one of the least important reasons for Cézanne's greatness.

Dorival, one of the most perceptive critics of Cézanne's work, noted that he came and went between Paris and Aix throughout his life, in particular when he went back to his native country, where his strength seemed to be renewed. He compared him to Antaeus, the giant of Greek mythology, who was invincible when his feet were touching the ground but weak when he lost contact with it. Hercules vanquished him by carrying him off — by depriving him with contact with the ground. Cézanne was Hercules and Antaeus in one: strong because he could stay in touch with the soil and strong because he could also leave it. In other words, instinct was as strong in him as was reason. He combined two major trends that alternate in the history of art as Classicism and Romanticism, or Classical and Baroque art, but which in a far-distant past were evinced in the civilisations and characters of great epochs. They are the Greek and Roman civilizations, rationalist and legalistic, which were opposed to the mystical

The Fruit Dish, ca 1885. Pencil and watercolor, 9⅜″ × 12½″ (23.8 × 31.8 cm)
Musée des Beaux-Arts, Budapest. Legs P. Majovsky

STILL LIFE WITH GREEN MELON, 1902-1906
Watercolor, 12⅜″ × 18¾″ (31.5 × 47.5 cm)
Private collection

civilizations of the Celts and the East; they are the Byzantine, Romanesque, and Gothic ages, which were opposed to the rationalism of the Renaissance. By evoking the ancient struggle between Antaeus and Hercules, Cézanne's work catches the essence of man's experience. Other artists, among the most remarkable, conjure up one or the other of these mythical figures, but Cézanne combines them both.

However, his complexity prevented him from deriving the maximum profit from the reduction of form to geometric shapes. His desire to simplify did not increase the three-dimensional effect as much as it could have, because he was too captivated by that which is irrational, richly unexpected in a fuzzy image, a warm confusion, and some complex twisting shapes: the baroque design in a tapestry (see p. 20), a writhing body (see p. 43), the folds of a table cloth (see p. 51), or a profusion of objects (see p. 50). He needed to invent another technique.

Which other technique? More aptly, where? He had worked long enough on objects; now he had to turn his attention to what surrounded them. In other words, he began thinking about perspective. What is the purpose of perspective? Its purpose is to create the impression that a painting is not a flat surface but a deep space. How does this space affect solid masses? He already knew how to isolate these masses to such a point that the eye sees them and nothing else; they cease to surprise and to draw our attention to the picture. In other cases, this space can vie with the masses, becoming a kind of inverse, concave mass, which makes the smaller, convex masses that it engulfs seem insignificant. An apple thrown into a space, the depth of which is too striking, becomes a small flat dot. Placed against a wall, however, it takes on a remarkable relief. It is a round surface welded to a flat surface, a bas-relief, which is so characteristic of Cézanne's painting. Bas-relief does not exclude depth, it only limits it. This limited depth is Cézanne's fourth technique to emphasize volume.

Limitation does not mean exclusion. Cézanne accused Gauguin of outrage against depth. He reproached him with showing a flat world altogether without depth. He took care not to fall into that which he regarded as an error, he wanted to create an impression of depth, but a moderate one. That is why he did not use very radical techniques. He avoided such strong techniques as the linear perspective and its convergence of lines that makes the distance look like the

▷

THE VASE OF TULIPS, 1890-1894
Oil on canvas, 23½" × 16⅝" (59.6 × 42.3 cm)
The Art Institute, Chicago. Collection of Mr. and Mrs. Lewis L. Coburn

L'ESTAQUE, 1898
Oil on canvas, 28¾″ × 35¾″ (73 × 91 cm)
Museu de Arte, São Paulo, Brazil

Montagne Sainte-Victoire
seen from the Bibémus Quarry, ca 1897
Oil on canvas, 25½″ × 32″ (64.8 × 81.3 cm)
The Baltimore Museum of Art
Gift of Miss Etta and Dr. Claribel Cone

75

◁

PORTRAIT OF MADAME CÉZANNE IN RED, ca 1890
Oil on canvas
35″ × 27½″ (89 × 70 cm)
Museu de Arte, São Paulo, Brazil

APPLES, BOTTLE, CHAIR BACK, 1902-1906
Pencil and watercolor on white paper
17½″ × 23¼″ (44.5 × 59 cm)
Courtauld Institute Galleries, London

77

Portrait of the Artist
Charcoal, 5″ × 8¾″ (12.7 × 22.2 cm) sheet
Sketchbook
The Art Institute, Chicago

bottom of a well. He preferred such methods as the breaking up of a detail in the foreground. In the portrait of his son (see p. 62), part of a canvas is visible, apparently placed on an easel; the easel cannot be seen but it is there in the viewer's imagination. It is there somewhere between the viewer and the picture, and it creates a distance between itself and the picture. This distance, however, can only be small. Cézanne also suggested depth with half-hidden objects. In his still lifes, for example, some apples partially hide other apples, leading to believe that the former stand behind the others. Finally, depth could be evoked by tapered shapes. In *The Cardplayers* (see p. 38), the head of the peasant standing against a wall is much smaller than that of the players. But since he is wearing a red scarf, the color of which explodes among the picture's other colors and burns itself in our vision, he seems to be just as near as the people in the foreground. One technique to create depth is canceled out by another.

In some cases, depth is both created and canceled out by the same technique. In *Large Pine* (see p. 82), depth is suggested by two oblique lines running contrary to each other, one running down from left to right and the other running up from right to left. The movement of these two lines produces a contrast and an impression of distance. But they join up and create a link between that which they seemed to separate. One might also wonder whether the great pine is tall because it is nearer than the other trees or because it is surrounded by shrubs. Its foliage and that of the other trees are treated in the same manner, as if they were equally near or far away.

Cézanne said, "I try to achieve perspective solely through color." Should this perspective through color be only a relief through color spread over the whole canvas, the results would be very limited. Nevertheless, warm colors — orange, for example — should give the impression of being slightly nearer than cool colors such as blue. What did Cézanne do? Look at his *Self-Portrait* (see p. 31). He attired himself in blue and placed himself in front of some orange-colored wainscoting, reversing again the order of colors. As a result, the wainscoting seems to overlap the figure of himself. Even when he abides by the correct order of colors and paints *Madame Cézanne in Red* (see p. 76) on a blue background, the blue is so light that it stands out as much as the model and seems to be part of the figure. In his landscapes, the sky — that infinite depth — ought to create an impression of vast distance. Cézanne, however, reduced the sky to a mere strip, using a plunging viewpoint with the earth filling most of the field of vision, or he made sky and earth merge, as in *Montagne Sainte-Victoire* (see p. 75). The sky then becomes like a huge wall swarming with solid masses, as in a Baroque bas-relief.

Portrait of Madame Cézanne, ca 1883
Black stone drawing
Boymans Museum, Rotterdam

In other words, Cézanne is the painter of distance that seems near. In his day, cyclists were acrobats and trains were the only rapid means of transportation that he knew. He never drove a car, and yet he saw things rather as a motorist does when compelled by sheer speed to consider distant objects as very near. Yet another reason why he is our kindred spirit. His concept of space, however, is modern in another sense. By dint of painting rocks and trees closely merged into one another, of seeing them purely as masses, he

BATHER, ca 1885.   Pencil and watercolor
8¾″ × 6⅝″ (22.2 × 17 cm)
The Wadsworth Atheneum, Hartford, Connecticut
Collection Ella Gallup Sumner and Mary Catlin Sumner

THE LARGE BATHERS, 1899-1906
Oil on canvas, 81⅞″ × 98″ (208 × 249 cm)
Philadelphia Museum of Art
Collection W.P. Wilstach

▷

LARGE PINE, 1892-1896
Oil on canvas, 33½″ × 36¼″ (84 × 92 cm)
Museu de Arte, São Paulo, Brazil

BIBÉMUS QUARRY, ca 1898
Oil on canvas, 25⅝″ × 21¼″ (65.1 × 54 cm)
Private collection, Los Angeles

◁

GIRL WITH DOLL, 1902-1904
Oil on canvas
28¾″ × 23⅝″ (73 × 60 cm)
Private collection

LEAVES IN A GREEN VASE, 1890-1892
Watercolor, 20″ × 13″ (50.7 × 33 cm)
Collection: Mr. and Mrs. Paul Hirschland
Great Neck, New York

succeeded in painting objects the size of which cannot be assessed anymore. One does not know whether there are small rocks seen from very near or big rocks seen from afar, shrubs at arm's length or trees miles away. The painting takes on different characteristics according to one's interpretation. This space as we see it in abstract paintings, in which shapes are close or remote depending on that which one imagines they could represent.

THE NAIVE VISION

"I should like to finish off this man's pictures," said Le Douanier Rousseau, speaking of Cézanne. It is true that Cézanne did not always finish his pictures. Quite often a patch of unpainted canvas would peer out from among the colors. This does not matter for true lovers of Cézanne. Renoir, who worked for a time with him in the Provence, said: "Cézanne is admirable: He cannot put two dabs of color on to a canvas without them being perfect." Two dabs were enough. What does it matter that the rest is left unfinished?

Cézanne never traveled much, in the ordinary sense of the word: Aix, his hometown, and its surroundings; Marseilles; Paris, where he often changed addresses; the Ile-de-France region; Lake Annecy and parts of Switzerland — he never went very far. Compared with Gauguin, who literally traveled the world, Cézanne seems a stay-at-home. And yet his work makes one feel that he has made a very long journey.

His two favorite themes, apples and Montagne Sainte-Victoire, have a mythical grandeur, taking us back to the misty dawn of time. Cézanne's apples have something so mysterious, such a strange texture, that they evoke the apples of the tree of knowledge in the Garden of Eden.

Christ ascended a mountain to speak some of the most significant words of His ministry. Before Him, Moses had ascended another mountain to receive the Tables of the Law. From times immemorial, mountains and islands have symbolized the meeting of sky and earth. The Montagne Sainte-Victoire merging into the sky of Cézanne's paintings evokes a new Mount Sinai and God's secrets.

It is not only their common concept of painting as a bas-relief that brings Cézanne and Greco together, it is also that their pictures are imbued with a similarly mystical atmosphere.

It seems that toward the end of his life, Cézanne tried to make an ultimate journey back through time, to the birth of the world and original chaos. He said that he wanted his paintings to reveal "the geological roots of landscape." Indeed the world that he depicted in most of his work is a nascent world, forever beginning: nascent, this mass-weight still bound to the surface of the canvas. And this mass is of compelling interest to us, since our age sees in it an image

JOURDAN'S HUT, 1906.   Oil on canvas, 25⅝″ × 31⅞″ (65 × 81 cm)
Collection: Riccardo Jucker, Milan

PORTRAIT OF THE ARTIST, ca 1895. Watercolor, 11¼″ × 10⅛″ (28.2 × 25.7 cm)
Private collection, Zurich

of itself. Ours is an age when it seems that a new world is about to be born, a new land is about to be discovered, a new original chaos is to be crossed in which new forms of life are stirring. At the same time, our age feels attached to a tremendous past, incomparably longer than was supposed a few centuries ago. We also are still bound to a background.

What would be more moving, more beautiful than these ties? Cézanne multiplied them in his works, not only the ties between rounded and flat surfaces, but also between all components of the picture, different as they might be. Paul Valéry said that space was "laden with ties." This was the space in Cézanne's paintings — and Valéry probably did not notice it, enamored as he was of Degas's work. Cézanne found a powerful poetic expression to his desire to unite everything, when he spoke of linking "the shoulders of hills and the curves of women." His *Bathers* (see p. 81) are grouped in such a way as to echo, in their gestures and the outline of their bodies, the large isosceles triangle formed by the horizon and the converging oblique lines of the tree trunks. This may be one of the most strikingly powerful examples in the history of painting of the human figure linked with the landscape by the unifying force of a repeated simple shape.

Cézanne and Nietzsche were contemporaries: the father of modern painting and the deviser of the superman theory. Born in 1844, Nietzsche was Cézanne's junior by only five years. He was to die in 1900, six years before Cézanne. They never met. Nevertheless, Nietzsche may have guessed something about Cézanne when, in "Thus Spake Zarathustra," he described the three metarmophoses of the spirit and explained how "the spirit became camel, the camel became a lion, and, finally, the lion became a child." In Nietzsche's allegory, the camel stands for the courage to shoulder a heavy task. Cézanne had that courage, since his passion for color made it very difficult to express his feeling for volume. Nietzsche added, "As soon as it is loaded, the camel hastens toward the desert, his own desert." Throughout most of his life, Cézanne was a solitary man, infuriated by the very idea "that people could buttonhole him." Nietzsche explained that "the spirit becomes a lion in the depth of the desert. ... It wants to win freedom." Cézanne won the lion's freedom with regard to Classicism and even Impressionism. Whenever necessary, he was not afraid to darken his palette, contrary to the tenets of Impressionism. He was not afraid to renounce the classical concept of space suitable for shapes evoking sculpture in the round, and substitute for it the space of bas-relief. He was not afraid, even, to reverse in some cases the sacrosanct perspective of classical painters. In *The Vase of Tulips* (see p. 73), the table top rises much too steeply to conform to the rules. The thickness of the table top does not taper as it recedes from our view, as it should according to the rules — nor does the supporting part of the table. On the contrary, it seems to grow as the distance increases. The viewer does not see the vase from the same perspective as the table. It seems that, in order to look at the vase, Cézanne placed himself at exactly the same level as the vase, while he must have looked at the table from above; it is as if he sat down to look at the vase and stood up again to look at the table. This was obviously against the classical rule of the constant observation point. Cézanne was a lion in Nietzsche's sense and rules mattered little to him, whether rules of perspective or anatomy. Here, the third metamorphosis appears very clearly, that by which the lion becomes a child. "The child is innocence," Nietzsche wrote, "innocence and forgetfulness, a new beginning, a first movement, a sacred 'yes'."

Cézanne had the innocence, the childlike naiveté of a Douanier Rousseau. Cézanne's naiveté, however, was twofold: It was both a naiveté of imagination, like that of Le Douanier Rousseau, and of the eye. There is naïveté of imagination in his *Bathers* (see p. 81): The human body is shaped without a thought for anatomy, in order to fit into a system of isosceles triangles. There is naivete of the eye in *The Boy with a Red Jacket* (see p. 32): The arm is lengthened without any care for anatomy. It mattered little that the proportions of the human body demand a shorter arm. What Cézanne knew before he looked did not matter, only that which he learned while looking. Cézanne strove for a pure, innocent vision of the world. He spoke of the need to "paint a bunch of carrots naively," of listening only to "that which our eyes think." We have preconceptions about what we see, and they influence our sensations. Cézanne believed in his own sensations, and he reproduced them as faithfully as possible by means of his technique with color and volume. The attention focused on the arm of *The Boy in the Red Jacket* gives this arm a considerable importance. He felt that it was bigger and longer — and that is how he painted it.

This fresh, naive vision of Cézanne is, for the lover of painting and the artist alike, that which the Canato fountain was for the goddess Juno: Every year she

Trees.   Albright-Knox Art Gallery, Buffalo, New York

made a pilgrimage to the fountain and bathed into its water, which gave her back her virginity.   This is the reason why there will always be pilgrimages to Cézanne's works, scattered as they are around the world.   There will always be homages to that man, who was stoned by the children of his hometown.   The children did not know that he was one of the greatest painters of all time and that he had kept intact the most precious quality of youth.

BIOGRAPHY

1839   Born on January 19, at Aix-en-Provence. His father's family had come from Italy in the middle of the 18th century. His father, a hatter who became a banker in 1947, did not marry Cézanne's mother until 1844.

1841   His sister Marie was born on July 4. She never married and she was to play an important role in Cézanne's life.

1844   Enrolled at the elementary school on the Rue des Epinaux at Aix.

1847-1848   His father took over the faltering Banque Bargès and, with his associate Cabassol, created the successful Banque Cézanne et Cabassol. His family's affluence was to free Cézanne of the need to sell paintings to make a living.

1849   Day student at the catholic school of Saint-Joseph.

1852   Entered Collège Bourdon, a catholic boarding school, where he met Emile Zola and Baptistin Baille. Both became longstanding friends. At the time, Cézanne was mostly interested in literature and poetry.

1854   His sister Rose was born.

1856   He began studying painting in the studio of Joseph Gibert at the Museum of Aix. He discovered Wagner's music and played in an orchestra with Zola. First known painting: *The Poet and His Muse.*

1858   Graduated from high school with honors and was awarded second prize for drawing at the Museum's school.

1859   At his father's request, he enrolled in law school at the University of Aix. His father bought an estate outside Aix, "Jas de Bouffan." Cézanne spent his summers there and built a studio.

1860-1862   With the support of his mother and sister Marie, Cézanne persuaded his father to allow him to become a painter. In April 1861, he went to Paris and enrolled at the Académie Suisse, where he met Armand Guillaumin and Camille Pissarro. He was disheartened by his failure at the entry examination for the Ecole des Beaux-Arts, and in September he returned to Aix to work in his father's bank. But he took evening classes in drawing. In November 1862, he returned to Paris and the Académie Suisse. Met Francisco Oller, Antoine Guillemet, Frédéric Bazille, Claude Monet, Alfred Sisley, and Auguste Renoir.

1863   Exhibited at the Salon des Refusés, although his name is not mentioned in the catalogue. Painted in chiaroscuro and admired Gustave Courbet, Edouard Manet, and Eugène Delacroix.

1864-1870   He divided his time between Paris and the Provence. None of his paintings was accepted at the Salon. Zola dedicated his "Confession de Claude" to Cézanne, who is mentioned for the first time as a painter in a review of Zola's book.

1866   Met Manet, who likes his still lifes.

1869   Met Hortense Fiquet, a nineteen-year-old model.

1870   At the onset of the Franco-Prussian war, he took refuge at L'Estaque, near Marseilles, with Hortense Fiquet.

1871   Returned to Paris.

1872   His son Paul was born on January 4. Without his father's knowledge, he settled with Hortense and son at Saint-Ouen-l'Aumône, near Pissarro and his family. Cézanne and Pissarro painted together in the open air, and Pissarro's influence proved to be very important for Cézanne's development. In September he moved for two years to Auvers-sur-Oise, where he lived with Dr. Gachet, who was at the time one of the few lovers and collectors of modern art.

1873   Landscapes of Pontoise and Auvers. Etchings. He met Vincent van Gogh and Père Tanguy. The latter opened a gallery in the Rue Clauzel in Paris and for a long time he was the only dealer to show Cézanne's work. Gachet bought several paintings.

1874   Took part in the first Impressionist exhibition at Nadar's. His works were singled out for the public's harshest criticism.

1875   Met Victor Chocquet, a civil servant and art collector, who later passionately defended Cézanne.

1876   In the south of France. He was not accepted at the Salon but he refused to exhibit at the second Impressionist show because he did not feel close enough to the group.

1877   Painted at Auvers and Pontoise. Took part for the last time in an Impressionist exhibition, where his paintings met with violent reactions.

1878   Settled with his family at L'Estaque. His father found out about his wife and reduced his financial support.

1879   Moved to Melun, near Paris, where he spent time with Zola.

1880   Moved to Paris, where he met Joris-Karl Huysmans and the followers of the Naturalist School. Summer with Zola at Médan.

1881   Stayed with Pissarro at Pontoise, where he met Paul Gauguin. He returned to Aix in November.

1882   Stayed at L'Estaque, where Renoir visited him. As a result of Guillemet's support, one of his paintings was accepted at the Salon. He settled at "Jas de Bouffan."

1883   Traveled in the Provence. Visited by Renoir and Monet.

1884   Stayed briefly with Renoir at La-Roche-Guyon. Later he returned to Provence, mainly to Gardanne, a hill town in the center of the coal-mining district near Aix.

1886   Zola published "L'Œuvre," the principal character of which was modeled on Cézanne and depicted a failed genius who ended up committing suicide. Cézanne broke with Zola and they never met again. With his father's consent, he married Hortense Fiquet in spite of their estrangement. Shortly thereafter, his father died, leaving him a considerable fortune.

1887   Worked in Aix. He exhibited at the Salon des XX in Brussels.

1888   Stayed for five months in Chantilly, where he painted the alleys to the castle and the banks of the Marne river. Met up again with Van Gogh and Gauguin, but he did not care for Gauguin's work.

1889   Settled at Aix. Visited by Renoir. He exhibited at the Décennale.

1890   Three paintings at the Salon des XX in Brussels.

1891   Toured Switzerland with his family. This was to be his only trip abroad. First symptoms of diabetes.

1892-1893   Worked in Aix and Fontainebleau, near Paris. He painted five versions of the *Cardplayers*, a series of *Bathers*, and a series of *Montagne Sainte-Victoire.*

1894   In the fall, he stayed with Monet at Giverny, where he met Auguste Rodin, Georges Clémenceau, and the art critic Gustave Geffroy. It is said that he threw himself at Rodin's feet, thus paying the great master a homage that he himself had been denied. Geffroy was to become one of his most fervent supporters. The Caillebotte bequest to the French National Collection included two paintings by Cézanne.

1895   First one-man show at the Ambroise Vollard gallery in Paris. His work was well received by art critics and collectors.

1896   Took the waters at Vichy. He stayed on Lake Annecy, where he met the young poet Joaquim Gasquet.

1897   His mother died on October 25. He worked near Aix.

1898   Stayed in Paris and Pontoise. His wife and son settled in Paris.

1899   Three paintings at The Salon des Indépendants. He regretfully sold "Jas de Bouffan" and settled in an apartment in Aix, under the care of a housekeeper and his sister Marie.

1900   Exhibited at the Centennale. His fame was spreading and the National Gallery in Berlin bought one of his landscapes.

1901   Exhibited at the Salon des Indépendants in Paris and the Salon de la Libre Esthétique in Brussels. Maurice Denis presented his own *Homage to Cézanne*, where the painter is shown surrounded by a group of young artists, Maurice Denis, Odilon Redon, Ker-Xavier Roussel, Paul Sérusier, and Edouard Vuillard. Cézanne bought a plot of land north of Aix to build a studio.

1902   The death of Zola moved him deeply. Cézanne is denied the Legion of Honor.

1904   Last stay in Paris. A whole room at the Salon d'Automne is devoted to his work. Cézanne had triumphed. Nine paintings at the Salon de la Libre Esthétique in Brussels.

1905   Exhibited at the Salon d'Automne and the Salon des Indépendants. He finished his *Large Bathers*, on which he had been working for seven years.

1906   Ten paintings at the Salon d'Automne. Cézanne died from a stroke on October 22.

1907   Retrospective exhibition at the Salon d'Automne, with fifty-six paintings.

BIBLIOGRAPHY

CATALOGUES RAISONNÉS

CHAPPUIS, Adrien. *The Drawings of Paul Cézanne, a catalogue raisonné.* London: Thames & Hudson. Greenwich, Connecticut: New York Graphic Society, 1973.

REWALD, John. *Paul Cézanne. The Watercolors. A Catalogue Raisonné.* Boston: Little, Brown, 1983.

VENTURI, Lionello. *Paul Cézanne: Son art, son œuvre.* 2 vols. Paris: P. Rosenberg, 1936.

Carnets de dessins. Préface et catalogue raisonné de John Rewald. Paris: Quatre Chemins, 1951. *Sketchbooks 1875-1885.* Tr. by Olivier Bernier. Introduction and catalogue by John Rewald. New York: Harcourt, Brace, Jovanovich, 1982.

WRITINGS BY CÉZANNE

Correspondance. Ed. by John Rewald. Paris: Grasset, 1937. Rev. ed., Grasset, 1978. *Letters.* Tr. by Marguerite Kay. London: Cassirer, 1941. Tr. by Seymour Hacker. New York: Hacker Art Books, 1976, 1983.

Lettere di Paul Cézanne. Ed. by Duilio Morosini and Ernesto Treccani. Milan: Valentino Bompiani, 1945.

Conversations avec Cézanne. Ed. by Yves-Alain Bois and Jean Clay. Paris, 1978.

BOOKS ON CÉZANNE

ADRIANI, Götz. *Paul Cézanne. "Der Liebeskampf," Aspekte zum Frühwerk Cézannes.* Munich: Piper, 1980.

ADRIANI, Götz. *Paul Cézanne. Aquarelle.* Cologne: DuMont, 1981.

ANDERSON, Wayne. *Cézanne's Portrait Drawings.* Cambridge, Massachusetts: The MIT Press, 1970.

ARROUYE, Jean. *La Provence de Cézanne.* Aix-en-Provence: Edisud, 1982.

AUZAS, Pierre-Marie. *Peintures de Paul Cézanne.* Paris: Chêne, 1946.

BADT, Kurt. *Die Kunst Cézannes.* Munich: Prestel, 1956. *The Art of Cézanne.* Tr. by Sheila Ann Ogilvie. Berkeley and Los Angeles: University of California Press, 1965.

BADT, Kurt. *Das Spätwerk Cézannes.* Constance: Universitätsverlag, 1971.

BARNES, A.C. and DE MAZIA, V. *The Art of Cézanne.* New York: Harcourt & Brace, 1939. Merion, Pennsylvania, 1977.

BARSKAYA, Anna Grigorieva. *Paul Cézanne.* Leningrad: Aurora, 1975.

BELL, Clive. *Since Cézanne.* New York: Harcourt & Brace, 1923.

BERNARD, Emile. *Souvenirs sur Paul Cézanne et Lettres.* Paris: Société des Trente, 1912, 1921. Paris: R.G. Michel, 1925.

BERNHEIM-JEUNE. *Cézanne.* Paris, 1914.

BHERTHOLD, Gertrude. *Cézanne und die alten Meister.* Stuttgart: Kohlhammer, 1958.

BEUCKEN Jean de. *Un Portrait de Cézanne.* Paris: Gallimard, 1955. Tr. and adapted by Lothian Small. New York: Viking, 1962.

BIEDERMAN, Charles, Joseph. *The New Cézanne; from Monet to Mondrian.* Red Wing, Minnesota: Art History, 1958.

BRION, Marcel. *Paul Cézanne.* Milan: Fratelli Fabbri, 1971, 1972. English ed., tr. by M.P. Benedetti, 1972.

BOISDEFFRE, Pierre et al. *Cézanne.* Paris: Hachette, 1966.

BURGER, Fritz. *Cézanne und Hodler. Einführung in die Probleme der Malerei der Gegenwart.* Munich: Delphin, 1913.

CASSOU, Jean. *Les Baigneuses.* Paris: Quatre Chemins, 1947.

CHAPPUIS, Adrien. *Les Dessins de Paul Cézanne.* Lausanne: Mermod, 1937.

CHAPPUIS, Adrien. *Les Dessins de Paul Cézanne au Cabinet des Estampes du Musée des Beaux-Arts de Bâle.* Olten: Urs Graf, 1962.

CHAPPUIS, Adrien. *Album de Paul Cézanne.* Preface by Rosaline Bacou. Paris: Berggruen, 1966.

COGNIAT, Raymond. *Cézanne.* Paris: Tisné, 1939.

COPLANS, John. *Cézanne. Watercolors.* Pasadena and Los Angeles, California: Ward Ritchie, 1967.

COQUIOT, Gustave. *Cézanne.* Paris: Ollendorf, 1919.

COTTE, Sabine. *Cézanne.* Paris, 1974.

COUTAGNE, Denys, ed. *Cézanne ou la peinture en jeu.* Conference proceedings. Paris: Criterion, 1982.

DORAN, M., ed. *Conversations avec Cézanne.* Paris: P. Brochet, 1978.

DORIVAL, Bernard. *Cézanne.* Paris: Tisné, 1948. Tr. by H.H.A. Thackthwaite. New York: Continental Book Center, 1948.

D'ORS, Eugenio. *Paul Cézanne.* Paris: Chroniques du jour, 1930.

DURET, Théodore. *Histoire des peintres impressionnistes.* 4th ed. Paris: Floury, 1939. *Manet and the French Impressionists.* Tr. by J.E. Crawford Flitch. London: Richards; Philadelphia: Lippincott, 1912.

EICHMANN, Ingeborg. *Cézanne.* Prague, 1936.

ELGAR, Frank. *Cézanne.* Paris: Somogy, 1968. London, 1969. New York: Abrams, 1975.

ERPEL, Fritz. *Paul Cézanne.* East Berlin: Henschelverlag, 1973.

FAURE, Elie. *Paul Cézanne.* Paris: H. Fabre, 1910. Paris: Crès, 1923. Tr. by Walter Pach. New York: Association of American Painters and Sculptors, 1913.

FAURE, Elie. *Cézanne.* Paris: Braun, 1936.

FEIST, Peter H. *Paul Cézanne.* Leipzig: Seemann, 1963.

FRANK, Paul. *Cézanne, eine Biographie.* Reinbeck bei Hamburg: Rowohlt, 1986.

FRY, Roger. *Cézanne, A Study of His Development.* London: Hogarth Press, 1927.

GACHET, Paul. *Cézanne à Auvers. Cézanne graveur.* Paris: Les Beaux-Arts, 1952.

GASQUET, Joaquim. *Paul Cézanne.* Paris: Bernheim-Jeune, 1921.

GENTHON, Istvan. *Cézanne.* Budapest, 1964.

GEORGE, Waldemar. *Cézanne. Aquarelles.* Paris: Quatre Chemins, 1926.

GRABER, Hans. *Cézanne d'après les témoignages des étrangers et des proches.* Basel: Schwabe, 1942.

GUERRISI, Michele. *La Nuova Pittura.* Turin: Erma, 1932.

GUERRY, Liliane. *Cézanne ou l'expression de l'espace.* Paris: Flammarion, 1950.

HANSON, Lawrence. *Mortal Victory. A Biography of Paul Cézanne.* New York: Holt, Reinhart & Winston, 1960.

HANSON, Lawrence & HANSON, Elizabeth. *The Seekers: Gauguin, Cézanne, Van Gogh.* New York: Random House, 1963.

HOOG, Michel. *L'Univers de Cézanne.* Paris: Scrépel, 1971. *The Universe of Cézanne.* Tr. by Dinah Harrison. Woodbury, New York: Barron's, 1979.

HUYGHE, René. *Cézanne.* Paris: Plon, 1936.

IGEKAMI, Chuji. *Cézanne.* Tokyo: Shueisha, 1969.

JEDLICKA, Gotthard. *Cézanne.* Bern: A. Scherz, 1948.

JOSEPHSON, Rognar. *Konstcerkets födelse.* Stockholm: Natur och Kultur, 1940.

JOURDAIN, Francis. *Cézanne.* Paris: Braun, 1950.

KAWAKITA, M. *Cézanne.* Tokyo, 1957.

KLINGSOR, Tristan. *Paul Cézanne.* Paris: Rieder, 1923.

LANGLE DE CARY, Marteau de. *Cézanne.* Paris: Caritas, 1957.

LARGUIER, Léo. *Le Dimanche avec Paul Cézanne.* Paris: L'Edition, 1925, 1936.

LARGUIER, Léo. *Paul Cézanne ou le drame de la peinture.* Paris: Denoël & Steele, 1936.

LARGUIER, Léo. *Cézanne ou la lutte avec l'ange de la peinture.* Paris: Julliard, 1947.

LASSAIGNE, Jacques. *Cézanne après inventaire.* Paris: Fayard, 1937.

LECLERC, André. *Cézanne.* Paris: Hypérion, 1949.

LEM, F.H. *Sur le chemin de la peinture: Paul Cézanne.* Paris: Sept Couleurs, 1969.

LINDSAY, Jack. *Cézanne, His Life and Work.* London: Evelyn, Adams & Mackay, 1969. Greenwich, Connecticut: New York Graphic Society, 1969.

LHOTE, André. *Cézanne.* Lausanne, 1949.

LORAN, Erle. *Cézanne's Composition.* Berkeley and Los Angeles: University of California Press, 1943. Rev. ed., 1970.

MACK, Gerstle. *La Vie de Paul Cézanne.* Paris: Gallimard, 1938.

MC LEAVE, Hugh. *A Man and His Mountain: The Life of Paul Cézanne.* New York: Macmillan, 1977.

MANDER, Giovanni van. *Un Pittore e il suo romanzo (Cézanne).* Milan: Bietti, 1944.

MEIER-GRAEFE, Julius. *Paul Cézanne,* Munich: Piper, 1910, 1918, 1922, 1923. Tr. by J. Holyroyd-Reece based on fifth ed. London: Benn, 1927. New York: Scribner's, 1927.

MEIER-GRAEFE, Julius. *Cézanne und sein Kreis. Ein Beitrag zur Entwicklungsgeschichte.* Munich: Piper, 1911, 1920, 1922. London, 1929.

MEIER-GRAEFE, Julius. *Cézanne Aquarelle.* Munich: Marées, 1918.

MEIER-GRAEFE, Julius. *Cézanne und seine Ahnen.* Munich: Marées, 1921.

MIRBEAU, Octave, ed. *Cézanne.* Paris: Bernheim-Jeune, 1914.

MONNERET, S. *Cézanne et Zola, la fraternité du génie.* Paris, 1978.

MURPHY, Richard W. *The World of Cézanne.* New York: Time-Life, 1968.

NEUMEYER, Alfred. *Cézanne Drawings.* New York: Yseloff, 1958.

NEUMEYER, Alfred. *Paul Cézanne. Die Badenden.* Stuttgart: Reclam, 1959.

NOVOTNY, Fritz. *Paul Cézanne.* Vienna: Phaidon, 1937. Tr. by Antoinette Nordmann. New York: Phaidon, 1948.

NOVOTNY, Fritz. *Cézanne und das Ende der wissenschaftlichen Perspektive.* Vienna: Schroll, 1938, 1971.

NOVOTNY, Fritz. *Paul Cézanne.* Exhibition catalogue. The Hague: Dienst voor Schone Kunsten, 1956.

NOVOTNY, Fritz. *Cézanne.* London, 1961. Orienti, Sandra. *L'Opera completa di Cézanne.* Milan: Rizzoli, 1970.

ORS, Eugenio d'. *Paul Cézanne.* French tr. by Francisco Amunategui. Paris: Chroniques du jour, 1930.

PERRUCHOT, Henri. *La Vie de Cézanne.* Paris: Hachette, 1956, 1959.

PFISTER, Kurt. *Cézanne. Gestalt, Werk, Mythos.* Potsdam, 1927.

PLAZY, Gilles. *Cézanne.* Paris: Siloé, 1981.

PONENTE, Nello. *Cézanne.* Bologna, 1980.

RAMUZ, C.F. *L'Exemple de Cézanne.* Lausanne: Mermod, 1951.

RAMUZ, C.F. *Cézanne. Formes.* Lausanne, 1968.

RATCLIFFE, R. *Cézanne's Working Methods and Their Theoretical Background.* Unpublished doctoral dissertation, University of London, 1960.

RAYMOND, Jean. *Cézanne, la vie, l'espace.* Paris: Seuil, 1986.

RAYNAL, Maurice. *Cézanne.* Paris: Cluny, 1936. Geneva: Skira, 1954. Tr. by James Emmons. Geneva: Skira, 1954.

REWALD, John. *Cézanne et Zola.* Doctoral dissertation, Sorbonne, Paris. Paris: Sedrowski, 1936. Rev. ed., *Paul Cézanne, sa vie, son œuvre, son amitié pour Zola.* Paris: A. Michel, 1939. *The Ordeal of Paul Cézanne.* Tr. by Margaret and H. Liebman. London: Phoenix House, 1950. Rev. ed., *Paul Cézanne, A Biography.* Tr. by Margaret and H. Liebman. New York: Simon & Shuster, 1948.

REWALD, John. *Cézanne, paysages.* Paris: Hazan, 1958.

REWALD, John. *Cézanne, Geffroy et Gasquet. Suivi de Souvenirs sur Cézanne de Louis Aurenche et de Lettres inédites.* Paris: Quatre Chemins, 1959.

REWALD, John. *Cézanne: A Biography.* New York: Abrams, 1986.

RILKE, Rainer Maria. *Briefe über Cézanne.* Ed. by Clara Rilke. Wiesbaden: Insel, 1952. Francfort, 1977.

RIVIÈRE, Jacques. *Cézanne.* Paris, 1910.

RIVIÈRE, Jacques. *Le Maître Paul Cézanne.* Paris: Floury, 1923.

RIVIÈRE, Jacques. *Cézanne, le peintre solitaire.* Paris: Floury, 1933, 1936, 1942.

ROUSSEAU, Théodore. *Paul Cézanne (1890-1906).* Paris: Flammarion, 1953.

SALMON, André. *Cézanne.* Paris: Stock, 1923.

SAN LAZZARO, P. *Cézanne.* Paris: Chroniques du jour, 1938.

SCHAPIRO, Meyer. *Paul Cézanne.* New York: Abrams, 1952, 1962.

SCHILDT, G. *Cézanne.* Stockholm, 1946.

SCHMIDT, Georg. *Aquarelle von Paul Cézanne.* Basel, 1952.

SEVERINI, Gino. *Cézanne et le Cézannisme.* Paris: L'Esprit nouveau, 1921.

SHIFF, Richard. *Cézanne and the End of Impressionism.* Chicago and London: University of Chicago Press, 1984.

SIBLIK, Jiri. *Paul Cézanne. Dessins.* Prague, 1968. Paris, 1972.

STOKES, Adrien. *Cézanne.* Paris: Nathan, 1953.

TAYLOR, Basil. *Cézanne.* Middlesex: Hamlyn, 1961, 1968.

TWITCHELL, Beverly H. *Cézanne and Formalism in Bloomsbury.* Doctoral dissertation, State University of New York, Binghampton, 1983. Ann Arbor, Michigan: UMI, 1987.

VENTURI, Lionello. *Paul Cézanne. Water Colours.* London: Cassirer, 1943.

VENTURI, Lionello. *Four Steps Toward Modern Art: Giorgione, Caravaggio, Manet, Cézanne.* New York: University of Columbia Press, 1956.

VENTURI, Lionello. *Cézanne.* Tr. by R. Skira. Geneva: Skira; New York: Rizzoli, 1978.

VOLLARD, Ambroise. *Paul Cézanne.* Paris: Vollard, 1914. Rev. ed., Paris: Crès, 1924. *Paul Cézanne, His Life and Art.* Tr. by Harold L. Van Doran. New York: Crown, 1937.

VOLLARD, Ambroise. *Ecoutant Cézanne, Degas, Renoir.* Paris: Grasset, 1938.

WADLEY, Nicholas. *Cézanne and His Art.* London, 1975.

WALDFOGEL, Melvin. *The Bathers of Paul Cézanne.* Unpublished doctoral dissertation, Harvard University, Cambridge, Massachusetts, 1961.

WANATABE, Yasuko. *Cézanne.* Tokyo: Kodansha, 1980.

WECHSLER, Judith Glazer. *The Interpretation of Cézanne.* Doctoral dissertation, University of California, 1972. Ann Arbor, Michigan: UMI, 1981.

WECHSLER, Judith Glazer, ed. *Cézanne in Perspective.* Englewood Cliffs, New Jersey: Prentice Hall, 1975.

WEDDERKOP, Hans von. *Paul Cézanne.* Leipzig, 1922.

YOSHIKAWA, I. *Cézanne.* Tokyo, 1962.

ZAHN, Leopold. *Paul Cézanne. Aquarelles de paysages.* Baden-Baden, 1957. Paris, 1958.

ZEISHO, Atzonji. *Paul Cézanne.* Tokyo, 1921.

EXHIBITIONS

1965   *Cézanne. The Collection of Mr. and Mrs. Henry Pearlman.* Williams Proctor Institute, Utica New York.

1966   *Cézanne, Redon, Renoir.* Nagoya Chunichi Gallery, Tokyo.

1967   *Cézanne and His Contemporaries. The Mr. and Mrs. Henry Pearlman Collection.* Detroit Institute of Arts.
Cézanne. Watercolors. Pasadena Museum of Arts, California. Catalogue by John Coplans.

1971   *Aquarelles de Cézanne.* Bernheim-Jeune, Paris.
Cézanne. An exhibition in honor of the fiftieth anniversary of the Phillips Collection. Phillips Memorial Gallery, Washington, D.C. Museum of Fine Arts, Boston. Art Institute, Chicago. Introduction by John Rewald.

1973   *Sixteen Watercolors on Loan from the Collection of Mr. and Mrs. Henry Pearlman.* Paul Rosenberg Gallery, New York.
Cézanne. Watercolours and Pencil Drawings. Laing Art Gallery, Newcastle-upon-Tyne. Hayward Gallery, London. Essay by Lawrence Gowing. Catalogue by Robert Ratcliffe.

1974   *Cézanne dans les musées nationaux.* Orangerie, Paris. Catalogue by Michel Hoog.

Cézanne. National Museum of Western Art, Tokyo. City Museum, Kyoto. Cultural Center, Fukuoka.

1976   *Les Estampes de Cézanne et les autres graveurs de son temps.* Musée Saint-Just, Saint-Rambert-sur-Loire.

1977   *Cézanne. The Late Work.* Museum of Modern Art, New York. Museum of Fine Art, Houston, Texas. Catalogue by William Rubin ed.

1978   *Cézanne. Les dernières années.* Grand Palais, Paris.
Paul Cézanne. Kunsthalle, Tübingen. Catalogue by Götz Adriani.

1979   *Disegni di Cézanne.* Palazzo Braschi, Rome. Catalogue by Nello Ponte.

1982   *Cézanne.* Musée Saint-Georges, Liège. Musée Granet, Aix-en-Provence.
Paul Cézanne. Aquarelle 1866-1906. Kunsthalle, Tübingen. Catalogue by Götz Adriani.

1983   *Paul Cézanne. Peintures, aquarelles et dessins.* Galerie Beyeler, Basel.
Cézanne in Philadelphia Collections. Museum of Art, Philadelphia.

LIST OF ILLUSTRATIONS